Mel Bay's *Beginning* FIDDLE SOLOS

by Stacy Phillips

MW01249055

ONLINE AUDIO

1 Put Your Little Foot [1:08]	16 Casey Jones [1:21]
2 Year of the Jubilo [1:42]	17 Jennie Lind Polka [1:14]
3 Black Eyed Susie [:48]	18 Down Yonder [1:02]
4 Life in the Finland Woods [1:12]	19 Cotton Eyed Joe [:35]
5 Too Young to Marry [1:20]	20 Goodbye Liza Jane [1:04]
6 Folding Down the Sheets [:58]	21 Joys of Quebec [1:05]
7 Texas Quickstep [1:21]	22 Take Me Out to the Ball Game [:58]
8 Cincinnati Hornpipe [1:54]	23 My Own House Waltz [1:08]
9 Make a Little Boat [1:14]	24 Hobo Jig [:48]
10 Rabbit Where's Your Mammy? [1:02]	25 Old Jaw Bone [1:05]
11 Little Brown Jug [:41]	26 Hogeye [:47]
12 Muddy Roads [:41]	27 Cluck Old Hen [:53]
13 Tombigbee Waltz [1:00]	28 Fire on the Mountain [:58]
14 Peas in the Pot [:53]	29 Granny Will Your Dog Bite? [1:22]
15 Poor Wayfaring Man of Grief [1:18]	30 Stone's Rag [1:09]

To Access the Online Audio Go To:
www.melbay.com/95590BCDEB

Visit us on the Web at www.melbay.com — E-mail us at email@melbay.com

Table of Contents

Introduction

This book contains a selection of fiddle tunes arranged for the beginning violin player. I have tried to avoid worn out war horses, and collected a sampling of melodies that will give almost instant gratification to the novice. (There is still *some* work involved!) One of the drawbacks of the classic way of teaching violin is the boredom of some of the early pedagogic repertoire. This book is meant to be an antidote to that tedium. Fiddle tunes are a great way to become accustomed with typical manipulations of major scales which are then applicable to all sorts of other music genres. The only technical prerequisite for this book is the ability to play the major scales of A, D, and G.

The tunes were chosen for their fun melodic content while demonstrating some typical aspects of fiddling. They are grouped by key with a couple of exceptions that are noted. Within each grouping they are ordered according to my vague idea of the challenge they might pose to the player.

I have minimized slurs. The few that are present are usually added to enable most measures to begin with a down bow. Fiddlers usually try to start most measures with a down, but the shape of the melody is the final arbiter. In any case, except where noted, slurring is not critical, so feel free to add occasional two note slurs if it makes a tune easier to play. Not too many though!

A note on the accompanying recording:

The recording that comes with this book is mixed with fiddle in one channel and guitar in the other. This will allow you to listen to the fiddle by itself, or avoid my wretched excesses entirely and use the guitar channel for karaoke play-along versions of the selections in this book.

I tried to stay as close as possible to the written notation but there are always some minor differences to be aware of, like the addition or omission of a slide or slur. Use of vibrato should be minimal in hoedowns, while extended notes in waltzes may be embellished with a relatively slow and narrow (compared to classical style) vibrato.

The music is recorded at relatively slow tempos; sufficiently fast to grasp the 'feel' of the tune but slow enough to be able to follow the written notation while you listen. Though the speeds are on the deliberate side, they are substantially quicker than you should first play a new piece. Begin by listening several times to an entire tune, then learn just a few notes at a time, playing the correct pitches and durations as slowly as needed to avoid mistakes. If you consistently make errors slow down.

The recording features Dave Howard on rhythm guitar and the engineering of Billy Sherr of Jack Straw Studios.

New Haven, Connecticut - July, 1995

Interpreting Notation

If you are not comfortable reading standard music notation; string and fingering position are indicated under each note. You can learn to read note duration from the accompanying recording.

The diagram shows the position of your fingers for a D scale. It begins with an open D string and, for the sake of illustration, continues past the octave D note. Notice how the fingering changes during the second octave on the E string.

FINGER POSITIONS ON THE VIOLIN FOR THE SCALE OF D

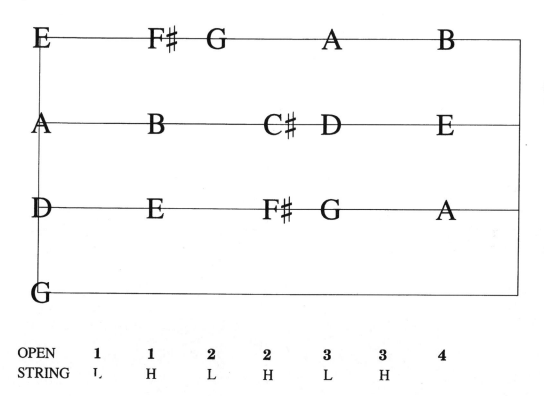

OPEN	1	1	2	2	3	3	4
STRING	L	H	L	H	L	H	

The corresponding music notation is:

5

All first finger placements in this book are high as in the diagram.

All third finger placements are *low* unless indicated otherwise. I usually indicate *high* and *low* information only when a finger changes its position during a tune.

1 = first finger, **2** = middle, **3** = ring, and **4** = pinky

"**H**" = *high* position and "**L**" = *low* position

Each time the bow switches strings the new string is identified in the fingering notation. Stay on the same string until a new one is notated.

The capital letters over the staffs are the chordal accompaniment.

Cut time meter ₵ can be treated the same as a fast 4/4 meter for our purposes. I used it in the unlikely case that a trained musician gets a gander at this book.

Andy Williams and Dave Milefsky at a festival in Elizabeth, West Virginia. Check out the various ways the fiddle and bow are held by the fiddlers pictured in this book.

(photo: Carl Fleischauer)

Put Your Little Foot

Let's begin with a couple of pieces that do not have a whole lot of notes. We'll ease into fiddle tunes one foot at a time. Tunes in 3/4 time are usually waltzes though a dance called a *varasovia* is often done to this melody.

The first bunch of tunes is in the key of D. In this key, the second finger plays in high position on the A, D, and G strings and in low position on the E string. The third finger plays low position on the E, A, and D strings and the first finger plays high on all four strings. (See the diagram in the "Interpreting Notation" section.)

Give a little thought to the fingering of the first two notes of measure 12 of *Put Your Little Foot*. Both the G and C♯ are played with the second finger but you must move up a half step (from *low 2 to high 2*) when you switch strings. Also, take care about the fingering of the first two notes of measure 10. The A and D utilize the same finger but on different strings.

Year of the Jubilo

Year of the Jubilo is a minstrel show-derived tune that makes for a fine hoedown or polka. It began as an anti-slavery song from the Civil War. The title refers to the biblical concept of the Jubilee Year when slaves were set free. While the lyrics are no longer performed, the melody lives on in the southern fiddle repertoire.

"Oh the master runs, ha ha!
And the freemen say 'Ho, ho!'
It must be now that the Kingdom's coming,
In the Year of Jubilo."

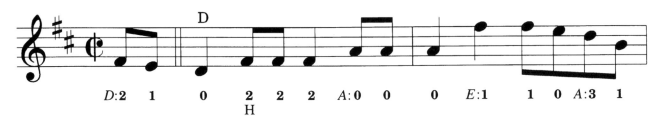

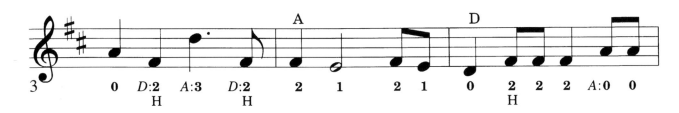

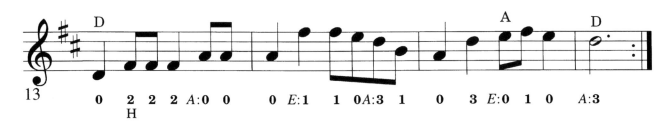

Black Eyed Susie

This pretty tune is based on a version by Doc Roberts, one of the greatest of the generation of old time fiddlers recorded in the 1920's. Much of his repertoire was learned from black fiddlers. The Afro-American string band tradition was quite popular in the South until it was gradually displaced by the blues in the early Twentieth Century. Its legacy is reflected in the repertoires of such as Roberts.

Note that there is one note not in the D scale; the G♯ in the first measure, played with the second finger in high position. (The G naturals in the lead-in and measure 3 are played in low position.) The two slurs in this piece serve to allow a down bow to begin most measures.

"Me and the boys went blackberry pickin',
We got sick and Susie got a lickin'.
Oh my pretty little black eyed Susie,
Oh my pretty little black eyed Susie."

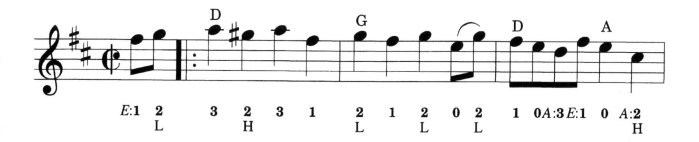

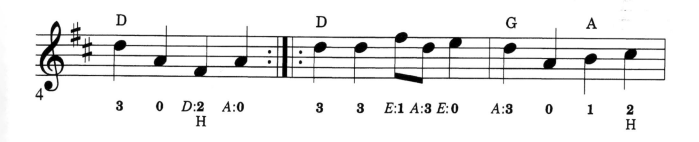

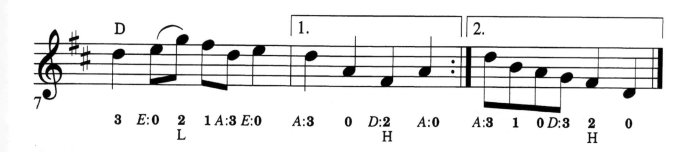

Life in the Finland Woods

The melody of this pert tidbit was heisted by the authors of "Mocking Bird Hill," which became an insipid pop hit for Patti Page in the colorless 1950's. Such recordings made rock and roll inevitable.

In measure 13, the first two notes are played with the same finger on different strings. You can always pick up the third finger after the D note and move down to the D string for the G note. Eventually I believe that you will find it easiest to cover the A and D strings simultaneously with that finger. You probably should not have to flatten your finger to cover both. The width of the top of the second finger is usually wide enough.

The first and second repeats are two measures long in each section.

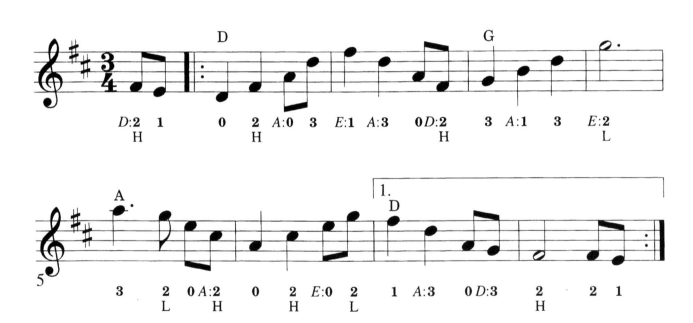

Life in the Finland Woods (continued)

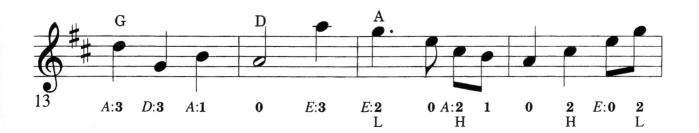

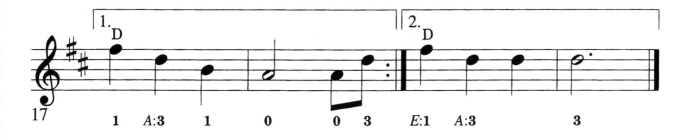

Too Young to Marry

    This Scottish-derived tune is a favorite of the contra dance world and somehow gained the name *Chinky Pin* in the American southeast. For square and contra dances, you need to pick a tune with two eight measure sections, each with very different melodies. This helps dance callers keep track of what step comes next while giving instructions. Some fiddlers like to switch the order of the sections and begin with my second section.

    Attention!! Measure 5 introduces the use of the pinky for a high B note. This is the weakest finger so it might take some weeks to build up its strength to the point that it can deliver as good a tone as your other fingers. Try keeping at least one additional finger on the strings when employing the pinky to help stabilize this weakling.

    This has got to be the tune with the most alternate titles. Among them are: *Chinky Pin, My Love She's But a Lassie, Buffalo Nickel, Ten Nights in a Bar Room,* and *Hair in the Butter.* There are many others.

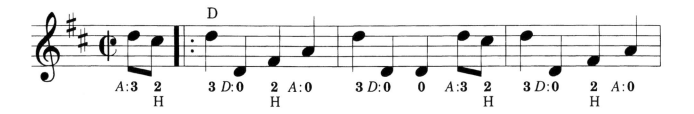

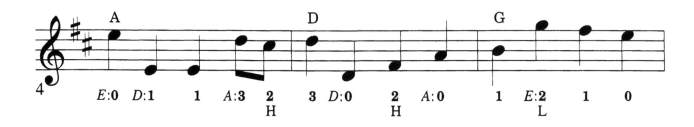

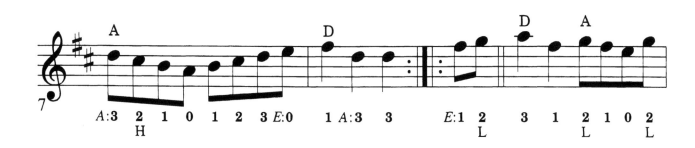

Too Young to Marry (continued)

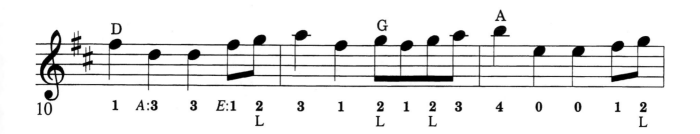

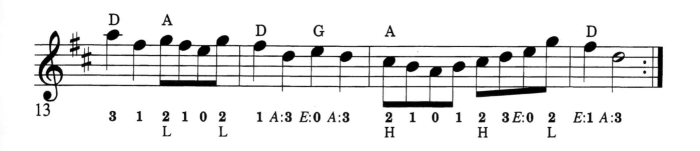

Folding Down the Sheets

Pay attention for the short *bow rocking* section between the A and D strings in the third measure. *Rocking* refers to alternating quickly between adjacent strings. The last note of the first section will probably come out on a down bow. Begin the repeat or next section with another down bow. The last note is held long enough to give you time to circle around with your bow.

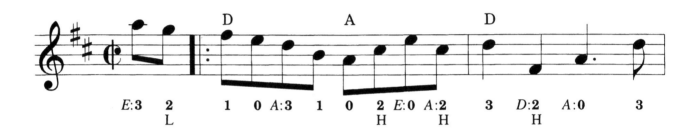

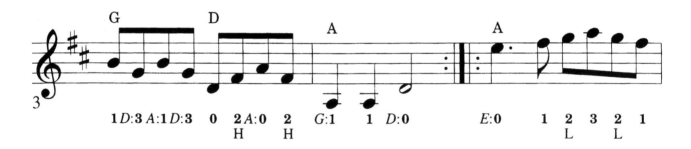

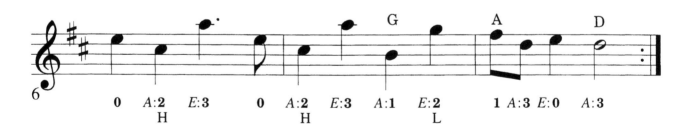

14

Texas Quickstep

This tune can be used for both a country dance and a polka. Watch out for the two measure repeats in the second section.

Cincinnati Hornpipe

Bow control is the major requirement of this tune. The chief motive here is rocking the bow between the A and D strings and then the E and A strings. When you get the speed up, the rocking motion will lend a propulsive rhythmic thrust to the tune. Though there are a lot of notes in this arrangement, many are open, so the fingering is not very demanding.

Hornpipes were originally played by shepherds on reeded animal horns and eventually became appropriated for some sort of sailor's dance.

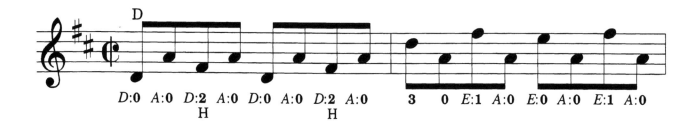

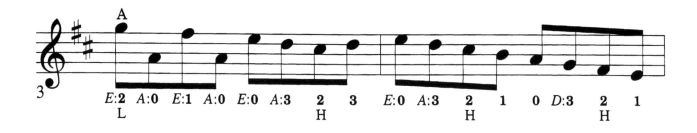

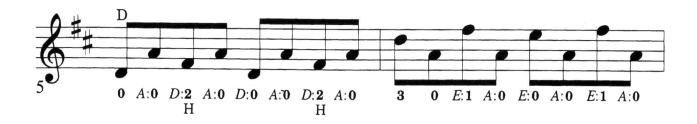

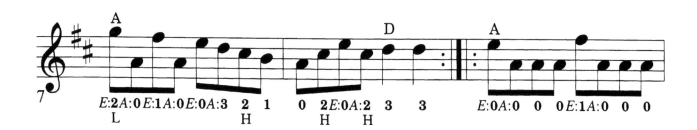

Cincinnati Hornpipe (continued)

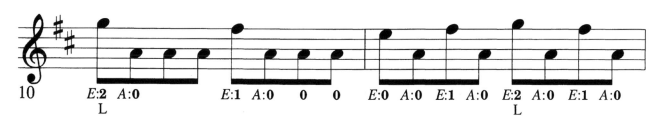

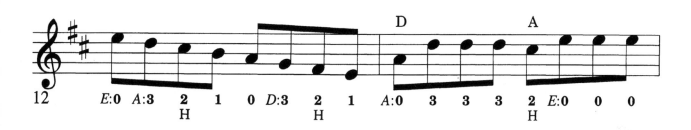

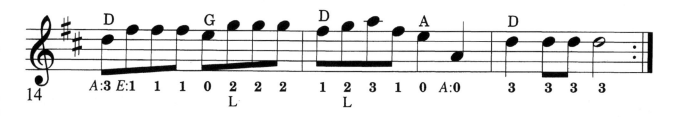

Make a Little Boat

Pay attention to the placement of the second finger in measures 2 and 6. That finger is placed in low position on the E string for the first note and the third note (C♯) is played in high position on the A string.

Measure 9 and 13 introduce a very challenging maneuver, a third finger stretch to high position (C♯) on the G string, followed by quick moves to the D then A strings.

Rabbit Where's Your Mammy?

This is the first tune in this book in the key of G. In this particular arrangement, all the fingerings are the same as in the key of D. (This is not so for most of the other key of G entries.) Check the diagrams in "Interpreting Notation" if you are unsure of placement.

"Rabbit where's your mammy?
Rabbit where's your mammy?
Rabbit where's your mammy?
She's down in Cincinnati."
(Probably doing a hornpipe.)

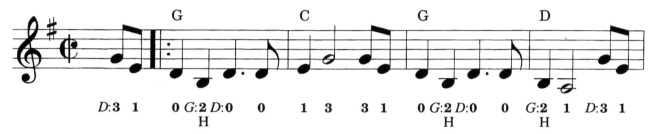

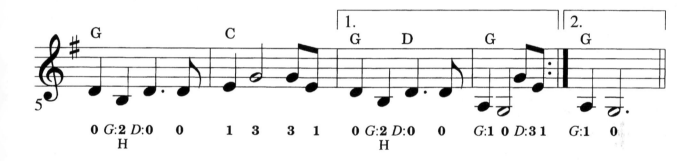

Little Brown Jug

This version of *Little Brown Jug* exhibits the kind of variation that a tune can undergo when operated on by fiddlers. I learned this Appalachian version of an old chestnut from a field recording of Brian Hubbard. It is a melody that benefits from hearing the accompanying chords.

Unlike the key of D, in the key of G the second finger is placed in low position on the A string. Does this tune switch to the key of D at the end of each section? Maybe. I don't care.

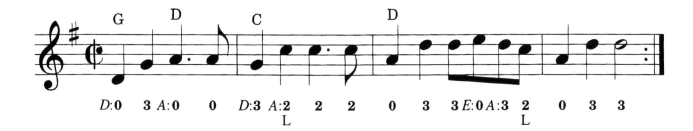

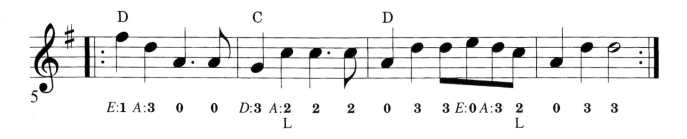

Muddy Roads

Though I have used the scale of D key signature, *Muddy Roads* uses a mix of the keys of D and G. Just pick and grin.

The one slur is added to measure 2 to make it easy to start the next measure with a down bow.

The accents are an important part of this tune. Increase the volume of an individual note by increasing bow speed. When you eventually increase the tempo to danceable speed (about 116 beats per minute on your metronome), the accents create a syncopation making dancing more fun.

"Going down the road, the road's so muddy,
I'm so drunk, I can't stand steady."

Tombigbee Waltz

This pretty tune is named for a river in Ohio. It demonstrates that a tune can be simple yet fun and effective. Whereas most fiddlers would guess that either the key of A or D are the most popular one for fiddle tunes, it turns out that there are more in G than any other key.

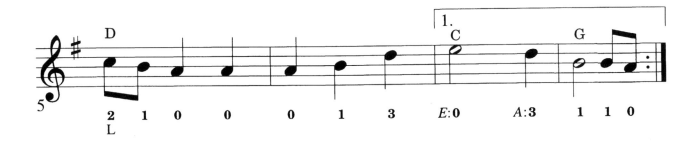

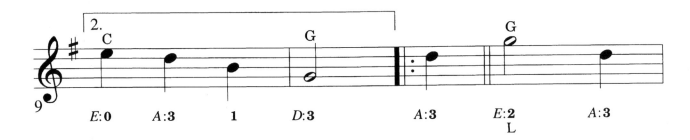

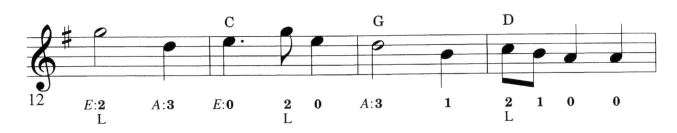

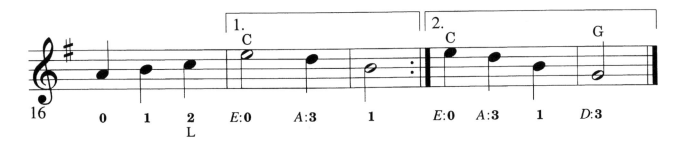

Bob Wills and Joe Holly, two important figures in western swing.

Peas in the Pot

I learned this twisted bit of a fluff from Clyde Davenport, an excellent purveyor of southeastern tunes on both fiddle and banjo. It sounds as if it came from the minstrel repertoire of the 19th Century. It is hard to tell where one phrase lets off and the next begins. This confusion is part of the charm of this piece.

The E note, beginning in measure 8, is held for a total of five beats. Make sure to save enough bow for the entire duration. Do not repeat the sections.

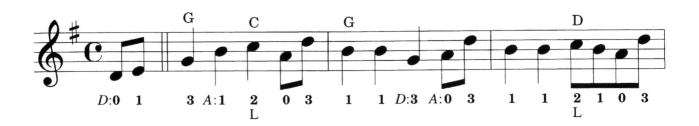

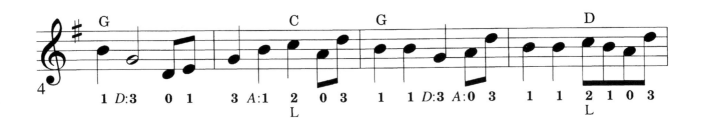

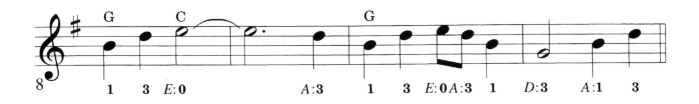

24

Peas in the Pot (continued)

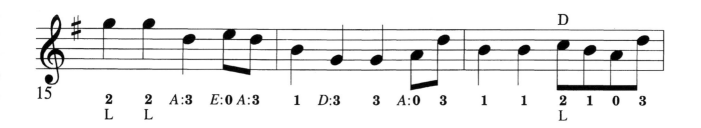

Poor Wayfaring Man of Grief

I learned this Utah waltz from the Deseret String Band. If you play it too slowly it sounds too pathetic. Try to work up to a brisk, danceable pace.

There are no repeats in this arrangement. The C note in the lead-in measure is the first *low* position third finger we have used on the G string. The 3's are low on every string in the key of G.

If the first D note in measure 24 comes out a down bow, play another down stroke on the following D. Alternately you might insert a slur.

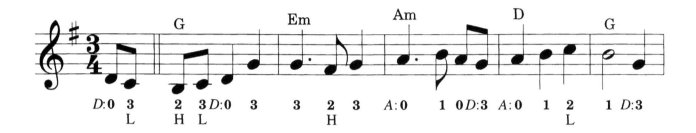

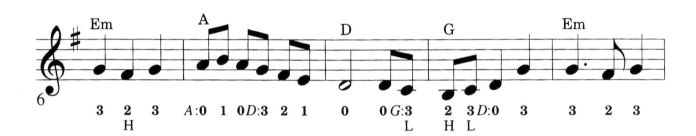

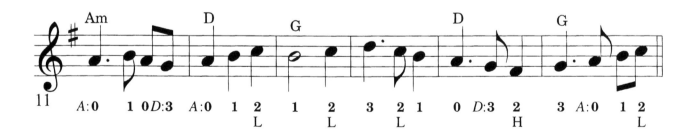

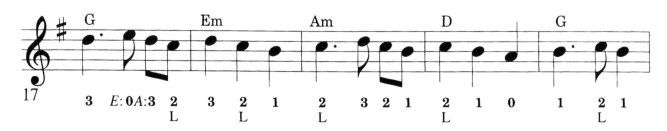

Poor Wayfaring Man of Grief (continued)

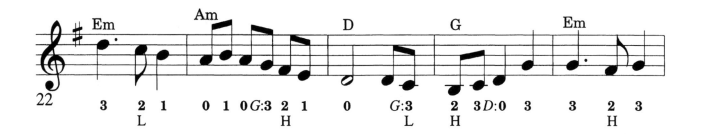

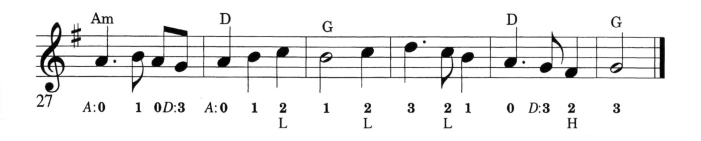

Casey Jones

    This rollicking folk ballad about the brave but doomed railroad engineer makes a great fiddle piece in the keys of D and G. This version is in G.

    There are many quick notes here but work up the tempo slowly. The stretches to the B notes in measures 10, 12 and 14 are particularly demanding in context. Keeping a finger on either/or the previous G and/or A notes may ease the use of your pinky muscles and also help guide you back to the correct pitches after the high B's. Try to avoid sliding into this pitch.

    In the next to last measure there are both *high* and *low* second finger positions.

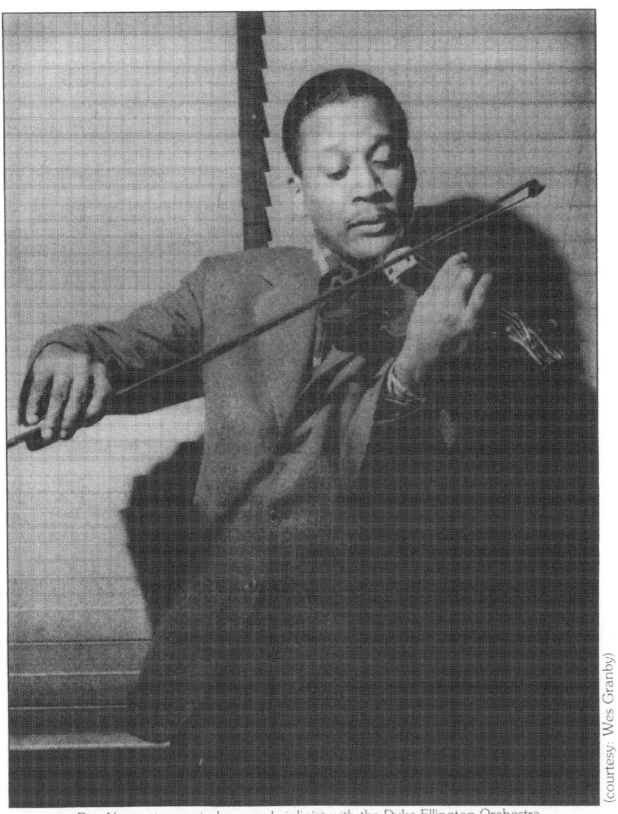

Ray Nance, trumpet player and violinist with the Duke Ellington Orchestra.

Jennie Lind Polka

This piece is named for the Swedish Nightingale, Johanna "Jennie" Lind (1820-1887), possibly the first intercontinental superstar. The greatest opera diva of her time, she had a vocal range from B below the staff line to G above high . What a show off! She inspired several of Hans Christian Anderson's stories, including "The Ugly Duckling." (Hans had a crush on Lind, but thought himself too plain-looking to attract her. Such is the sort of romanticism that makes effective writers of fairy tales.)

P.T. Barnum, possibly the first intercontinental humbugger, arranged a tour of America for Lind that blew the socks off the whole country. Among the offshoots of the resultant Lind-omania were compositions like this. A reel named for Lind also found its way into the fade out of Bill Monroe's famous song, *Uncle Pen*.

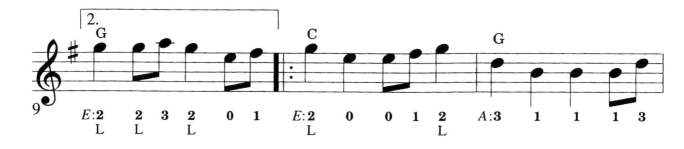

Jennie Lind Polka (continued)

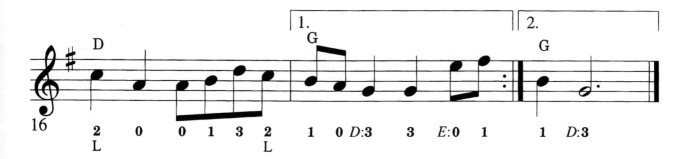

Down Yonder

This tune entered the fiddle world by way of the Skillet Lickers, one of the best, and wildest old time bands from the 1920's and early '30's. It immediately became a fiddle standard. Many of the southern string bands gave their groups this sort of humorous, self-deprecating name.

Down Yonder has a bit of a ragtime feel to it, especially in the syncopated rhythm of the melody in measures 1-4 and 9-12. It is imperative to get this right. Otherwise the tune will be flat and boring. This arrangement has both *high* and *low* 2s on the A string.

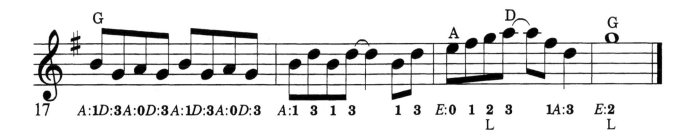

Cotton Eyed Joe

There are several completely different fiddle tunes with this title. This one was first recorded in the 1940's by Adolph Hofner's western swing band, featuring the wonderful jazz violinist J.R. Chatwell. It is the version that became connected with an insipid, pop-country line dance. Go figure.

This is our first tune in the key of A. For now there are no new fingerings. The title apparently refers to an eye condition resulting from imbibing impure moonshine.

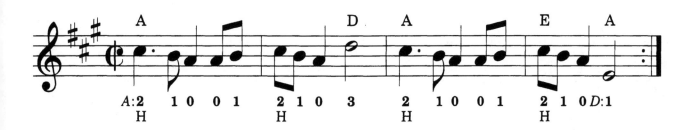

Goodbye Liza Jane

Goodbye Liza Jane is the first tune in this book to use *high* third finger position on the D string in measures 7 and 15. It is the same relative stretch as on the G string in *Make a Little Boat*. This tune was part of the Bob Wills western swing repertoire. I learned it by way of a fine album titled "Texas Crapshooter" by fiddler Bobby Hicks.

All the 2s are high in the key of A. There are a couple of high 3's in this piece.

"River's up and the channel is deep
A goodbye, a goodbye,
River's up and the channel is deep
Goodbye Liza Jane.
Oh, how I love her, Ain't that a shame.
Oh how I love her, Goodbye Liza Jane."

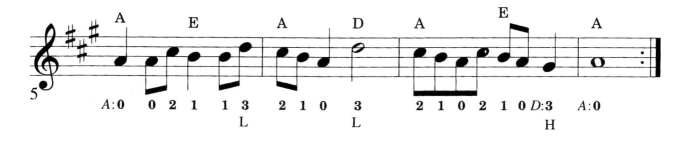

Joys of Quebec

French Canadian fiddle tunes have a certain *joie de vivre* that make them fun to play. *Joys of Quebec* is one of the most famous.

In measure 10, the first note (high A) will probably be a down bow. Make the following note (C♯) another down. Likewise in measure 18, the first note (C♯) will probably be a down bow, the second (also C♯) should also be down. This is done to make the next measure begin with another down bow.

Repeats in both sections are two measures long. (Remember that all the second finger positions are also high in the key of A.)

Take Me Out to the Ball Game

Everyone knows this tune but no one plays it outside baseball stadia. I have decided to induct it into the pantheon of country waltzes. It makes a fine fiddle tune.

In this arrangement, all the 3's are *low*. Let your accompanist worry about the D♯ diminished chord in measure 26. A plain old D chord would work, but would sound much less urbane. (By the way, every fiddler is entitled to refer to a *diminished* chord as a *demented* chord, but only once in your career. Pick your moment carefully.)

Old-time fiddlers at the Smithsonian Festival in Washington D.C.

(photo: Carl Fleischauer)

My Own House Waltz

The first section of *My Own House* is in the key of A and the second is in D. However, the tune is organized so you can play the second section with the exact same fingering as the first, **but one string lower.** This means, for example, that the melody begins (after the kickoff measure) on the A string. The second section begins with the identical fingering but on the D string.

All 2s are *high* and 3's are *low* in this arrangement. There are no repeats. On the recording, I put in a few slurs that are not notated. They are not necessary for a '"correct" rendition of this tune.

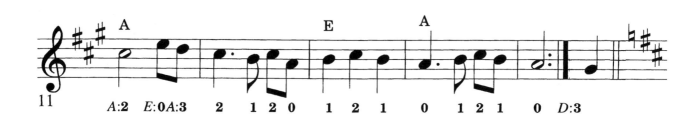

My Own House Waltz (continued)

Hobo Jig

In jigs, each ⅛ note is a beat, so they go by pretty fast. (In all the other tunes in this book, a beat is a ¼ note in duration.) There are six ⅛ notes per measure. Like *My Own House,* this piece switches keys, except that this one begins in D and ends in A. Watch out for the different *high* and *low* fingerings. All 3's are low in this piece, but the 2 positions vary.

Old Jaw Bone

Old Jaw Bone is in the key of A, although it mostly uses the same notes as a D scale. It is considered in the key of A because the final and most important chord is A. The resultant slightly exotic sound is usually referred to as a *modal* type old time tune. I will not try to define this term. Listen to the next four tunes on the recording and you will begin to recognize the style.

I learned this piece from the Carter Brothers and Son, a wild and distinctly non-commercial trio from the 1920's.

"Jaw bone walk and jaw bone talk,
And jaw bone eat with a knife and a fork.
I put my jaw bone on the fence,
I ain't seen nothin' of my jaw bone since.
Old jaw bone, Jimmy get along, here comes daddy with the booties on.
Old jaw bone, Jimmy get along, here comes daddy with the red dress on."

Hogeye

This is another key of A tune using D scale notes. The A chord to G chord move is typical of this class of music. It is also found in a great many Irish instrumentals. The phrase in measures 1, 3, 5, and 7 also appears in the versions of *Fire on the Mountain* and *Granny Will Your Dog Bite?* that follow.

All the 3's are *low* in this tune.

> "Sally's in the garden sifting, sifting,
> Sally's in the garden sifting sand.
> Sally's in the garden sifting, sifting,
> Sally's upstairs with the hog-eyed man."

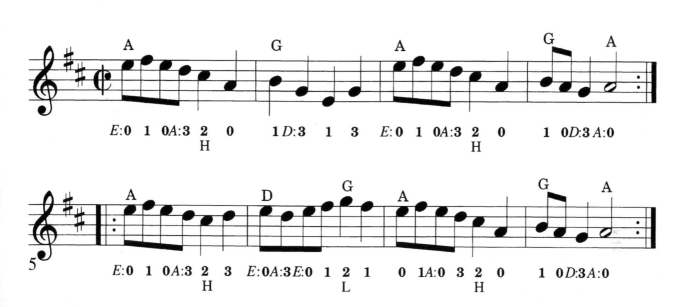

Cluck Old Hen

Continuing with our foray into the world of modal fiddle tunes, here is an example of the phylum: tunes - fiddle, subgenre: modal - farm animal imitation.

Pizz. means to pluck the given note (here the open E string) with your finger. It is probably easiest to use the ring finger of your **left** hand. *Arco* means to return to bowing. Play a down bow after each *pizzicato*. The plucking is supposedly in imitation of a hen's cluck. I wouldn't know. The only chickens that I have seen up close have been wrapped in clear plastic.

I learned this tune from Charlie Acuff.

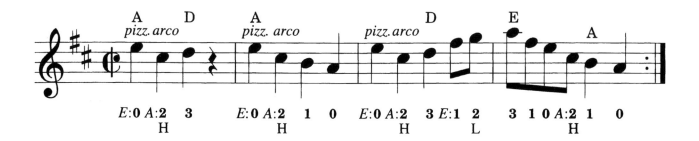

Fire on the Mountain

There are several related tunes with the same title. This version is not the most famous, but it has great character. Its odd length (for a traditional fiddle tune) means it cannot be used for square dances.

Watch out for both *high* and *low* third finger positions on the D string. The 3's on the other strings are all *low*. Note the different lengths of the repeats in the first section.

Granny Will Your Dog Bite?

This is one of the more difficult tunes in the book, with a number of third finger stretches on the G and D strings. Keep a lookout for the *low 2* on the E string in measures 10 and 14, and the *high 2* on the same string in measure 12. There are also demanding string change sequences that may test the limits of your technique.

"Chicken in the bread pan, kickin' up the dough,
Granny will your dog bite, no child no."

Joshua and Alexis Rooks, ace family fiddling team from Connecticut.

(photo courtesy of the Rooks family)

Stone's Rag

The high C note in measure 23 is probably the single most exciting note in this book. You may have to move your hand up the neck a bit to reach it. However, it is not uncommon to have sufficiently large hands to just stretch a bit with your pinky. The latter makes it easier to keep the following note in tune. As you can hear on the accompanying recording, a quick slide up to the high C is perfectly acceptable in fiddling. Just make sure you can hear the correct pitch in your head before leaping to this unprecedented altitude.

This is the only tune in the key of C. The only new pitch in this arrangement is a *low* 2 on the D string. Notice that the fingering on the D and A strings in measures 3-4 is almost the exact same thing as in measures 1 and 2 on the A and E strings. Likewise, measures 13-14 is the same as measures 11-12, just shifted down a string.

All the 2's and 3's in this version of *Stone's Rag* are low. There is no repeat of the second section. Like *Down Yonder*, the timing of the melody (specifically the many tied notes) are critical to the raggy feel of this piece.

An alternate title for this tune is *Forty Dogs in a Meat House*.

Stone's Rag (continued)

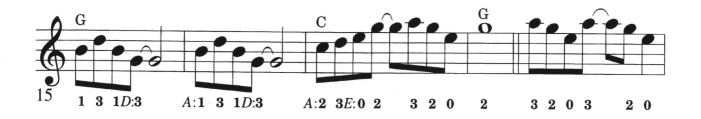

Other Books of Interest

Here is a list of my other books that may be of interest when you are prepared to reach for the next plateau. You can contact me about them through Mel Bay Publications.

Bluegrass Fiddle Styles - careful transcriptions of over 60 of the most influential bluegrass solos...Chubby Wise, Benny Martin, Vassar Clements, Richard Greene, Bobby Hicks, Paul Warren, Scotty Stoneman, Kenny Baker, Jimmy Buchanan, Byron Berline, etc. ...the book that tells the whole truth...includes analyses and historical background.

Mark O'Connor - The Championship Years - meticulous transcriptions of Mark's trend-setting performances at fiddle contests...written with Mark's help...major interviews and detailed analyses...the most influential fiddle style of the past fifteen years.

The Phillips Collection of Traditional American Fiddle Tunes...an unprecedented compendium of 1300 fiddle tunes......in two volumes (the first - hoedowns and reels, the second - rags, blues, listening pieces, polkas, hornpipes, jigs, waltzes etc.)...each entry based on the playing of an outstanding fiddler (over 300 represented) with multiple versions of many tunes...bowing, fingering and chordal accompaniment included.

Twin Fiddling - hip harmony arrangements for two and three fiddles in several styles...bluegrass, blues, western swing, Irish, etc....with explanation for creating your own harmonies.

Made in the USA
Middletown, DE
27 February 2021